PEAK RETIREMENT

The 5 Pillars to Protect Your Wealth and Live the Retirement You Deserve

JOE F. SCHMITZ JR. CFP®, ChFC®, CKA®

bestselling author of ***I Hate Taxes***

PEAK RETIREMENT

PEAK RETIREMENT

The 5 Pillars to Protect Your Wealth and Live the Retirement You Deserve

ISBN: 978-1-956220-93-3

Expert Press
1067 N Main Street #235
Nicholasville, KY 40356

www.ExpertPress.net

PEAK RETIREMENT

The 5 Pillars to Protect Your Wealth and Live the Retirement You Deserve

Joe F. Schmitz Jr.,
CFP®, ChFC®, CKA®

CONTENTS

Tax Planning

✓ Use of tax software, reports, and calculators
✓ Roth conversions
✓ RMD planning
✓ Charitable planning
✓ Tax prep

Investment Planning

✓ Seeking protection and growth based on your objectives
✓ Eliminating unnecessary fees
✓ Professional investment management

Income Planning

✓ Generate income from investments
✓ Social Security planning
✓ Pension planning
✓ Tax-efficient withdrawal strategy

Estate Planning

✓ Estate planning documents—trust, will, POA, etc.
✓ Survivor planning
✓ Reducing taxes to beneficiaries
✓ Purpose planning

Health Care Planning

✓ Medicare planning
✓ Long-term care strategies
✓ Planning for out-of-pocket expenses
✓ Planning for early retirement

Introduction

I was hosting a retirement workshop on our 5 Pillar Approach—which I've done hundreds of times—and something happened that has stuck with me. One of the attendees, John, now a client of ours, approached me afterward, shook my hand, and pointed to the slide of the retirement mountain, pictured on the next page. I'll never forget what he said. It encapsulates why I have built a firm that helps people create a comprehensive retirement plan.

He said, "Joe, this mountain analogy and the five pillars you discussed tonight are what I need help with. I don't want to make a stupid mistake with what I've worked so hard to accumulate over the last forty years. I've never planned a retirement before. I need help so I can live the retirement I've been dreaming of."

We built the 5 Pillar Approach for people like John: diligent savers who have worked hard to accumulate their

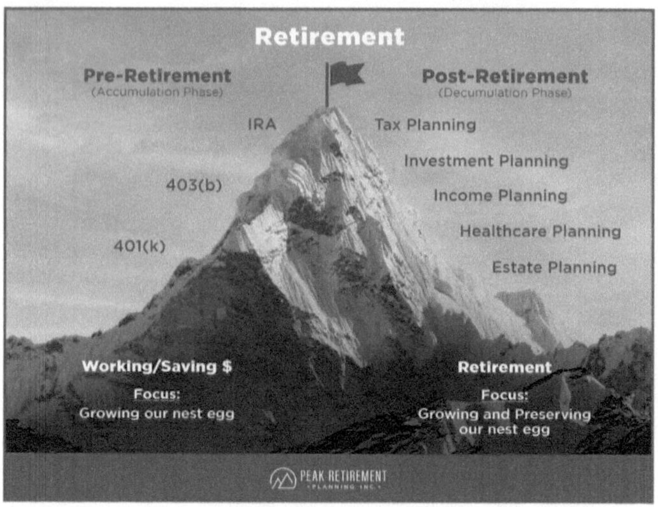

retirement savings and don't want to miss things that will negatively affect their finances in later years.

We describe many of the clients we work with as "Midwestern Millionaires." Why? Because most of our clients have midwestern values. They are diligent savers and hard workers, frugal, honest and conservative people. Those values have enabled these clients to build a net worth of $1 million or more as they plan for retirement, which requires help from a more advanced team. These are the people for whom our 5 Pillar Approach is most effective. I even wrote a book about this and it was a national bestseller.

They haven't built their net worth by making $1 million a year. They have done it by having good jobs, putting in the time and effort, and taking the right steps of saving and

spending less than they make. Now they are motivated to be the best possible stewards of their wealth and to avoid leaving money on the table. We often tell them, "You may not need more money at this point. You may just need a better plan."

John scheduled a Discovery Session with our firm to learn more about the 5 Pillar Approach. He told us what he wanted to achieve with our firm:

- To establish a Tax Plan to keep more money in his pocket and less in Uncle Sam's.

- To develop an Investment Plan that ensures he does not have to check it every day, research the investments he chooses, or worry about missing

opportunities. He was also worried about taking
on more risk than is necessary to accomplish
his goals.

- To create an Income Plan that provides a paycheck
for the rest of his life so he doesn't have to worry
about running out of money.

- To establish a Healthcare Plan that includes
the correct supplemental Medicare plans and
calculates for out-of-pocket healthcare expenses
or a potential long-term care need.

- To establish an Estate Plan that has all his estate
planning documents in place (powers of attorney,
wills, trusts, etc.) and takes care of his wife and
adult children when he passes away, ensuring they
pay the least amount of tax and avoid probate.

Our 5 Pillar Approach covers every one of John's
concerns.

At Peak Retirement Planning, Inc., we have a specific
process. We don't improvise when helping clients steward
their life savings. We focus on serving those in or near retirement, people in their fifties and sixties. Most of our clients
are diligent savers with substantial tax-deferred retirement

savings. They are attracted to our comprehensive focus on retirement planning and particularly tax planning (as you can see in another book I wrote, *I Hate Taxes*, an Amazon bestseller in the taxes and retirement planning categories).

As you will learn in this book, our process differentiates us from many financial planning firms. Other firms concentrate on investment planning, but investments are only one piece of the pie.

To have a complete financial plan, you need all five pillars of our 5 Pillar Approach:

1. Tax Planning
2. Investment Planning
3. Income Planning
4. Healthcare Planning
5. Estate Planning

Our boutique approach of working with a specific crowd and not trying to serve everyone means we're able to deliver on all five of these essential areas. We are also an independent retirement planning firm, which means we are not forced to push any specific investment or products. We sit on the same side of the table as our clients and help them decide what is best for them.

Our team approach also differentiates us and allows us to deliver this high-level service. Multiple eyes viewing each plan ensures we don't miss anything. Every team member is an expert in a specific area rather than a "jack-of-all-trades, master of none."

All our advisors are fully licensed fiduciaries and are either CFP® professionals or are in the process of becoming CFP® professionals. I have personally instructed each of our advisors in our intensive and extensive training program, all about maximizing financial situations for those in or near retirement. We stay educated on topics within the current financial environment so our clients can quickly take advantage of any opportunities that arise.

Part of our process is to meet with our clients at least annually, and more often if we need to. This allows us and them to adjust the plan for changes and do ongoing tax planning each year. We also personally reach out to them every quarter to add value to their plan and ensure we are not missing anything. We are available anytime to answer questions, and we always reply back to our clients within twenty-four hours. We update our client's investment portfolios as required.

Why am I sharing all of this? I started Peak Retirement Planning, Inc. because I saw too many gaps in the financial planning industry, and I saw too many people in or near retirement not getting the guidance they needed to enjoy the retirement they deserved. Retirees were missing out on having all of the five pillars working together in one place.

I have always thought that if you want to see a change, you make it yourself. So I did. I started on a mission at age twenty-five to build Peak Retirement Planning, Inc. into the organization it is today. People noticed that our service model was innovative, cutting edge, and different from most. In just over two short years, the business went from one person to twenty team members. I connected with close and trusted family and friends about working with me—when asked to get on a rocket ship, you get on, is what I told them. My first four hires were my mom, a friend since fourth grade, and two friends from college. They quickly understood Peak Retirement's mission and its impact. This was something special.

We've come a long way. One person alone could never do what our team has accomplished. Our success requires a dedicated and committed team, and particularly a group of clients, to trust our mission and then deliver on what we promise.

I'm writing this book to encourage you to work with a firm that does all the planning of our 5 Pillar Approach. Whether you work with us or someone else, make sure they work hard for you and provide a full service.

Note that these five pillars are interdependent. Preparing one of them without the others is incomplete planning and places your retirement at risk. Begin your retirement plan on the next page with Pillar 1: Tax Planning.

Chapter 1

Pillar 1: Tax Planning

Taxes will be the most significant expense in retirement, yet they are talked about and planned for the least. I could write a whole book about tax planning. Oh, wait. I already have. Read my book *I Hate Taxes* to get more insight on my favorite financial planning topic: taxes.

To be clear, I don't necessarily hate taxes. I'm not anti-American. I chose that title for the book because it's eye-catching, and people might feel compelled to read it. I do believe, however, that the US government isn't the best steward of our tax dollars.

I agree with certain things that my tax dollars are used for, like the roads I drive on and the libraries I go to. However, our government overspends on unnecessary things that don't always match my values and beliefs. Because of that, I would like to save taxes on the money I've worked hard for. I'd like to pay less tax all the time—especially if the tax code encourages me to do so and gives me opportunities to pay the least amount possible as long as I follow the rules.

Tax Planning is the first pillar in our retirement strategy because it's the cornerstone of everything we do at Peak Retirement Planning, Inc. But the pillars are interdependent. Taxes play a part in each of the other four pillars, and we plan accordingly:

- **Pillar 2: Investment Planning.** Ensure that your investments grow in a tax-smart way.

- **Pillar 3: Income Planning.** Ensure that your investments are taken out in a tax-smart way when you need to live off them in retirement.

- **Pillar 4: Healthcare Planning.** Ensure that you use your assets in a tax-smart way when paying for unexpected healthcare costs.

- **Pillar 5: Estate Planning.** Ensure that you leave your assets behind in a tax-smart way to your beneficiaries to make them the largest beneficiary (and not Uncle Sam).

Based on feedback from our clients, it is our first pillar that attracted them to work with us.

Most people have their retirement savings in tax-deferred investments like 401(k)s and individual retirement accounts (IRAs), which haven't been taxed yet. What happens when you withdraw funds from these investments? You must pay tax. This will increase your income and potentially force you to pay more taxes over time at expected higher tax rates since most experts suggest tax rates will increase.

Let me give you a rundown of what is essential for tax planning in your financial plan and what we look to accomplish with our clients.

Using Tax Software, Tax Calculators, and Tax Reports

Don't improvise when doing your tax planning. A deep analysis will determine what decisions you should make when taking income from your investments and deciding which tax planning strategies will best serve you. We typically spend at least ten to twenty hours building out a tax plan for our clients, considering not only what their taxes look like today but what they'll look like in the future.

We also examine all areas that affect taxes. We look at more than the federal income tax rates when making decisions. We must understand how our decisions will affect state taxes and the tax you could potentially pay on Social

Security when you start receiving your benefit in retirement. We must recognize the impact of capital gains and the increase in Medicare premiums when you have a higher income. We must also understand the effects of planning for other specific deductions and credits. And for those who have really done a good job saving, we must focus on the estate tax and any inheritance taxes.

At Peak Retirement Planning, Inc., we use advanced tax-planning software and calculators that produce in-depth and accurate reports that help us use our expertise to save our clients money on taxes over their lifetime. This is one reason we recommend you work with a professional—tax software can be expensive for an individual to buy independently and even more challenging to learn to use accurately. The tax savings alone is worth the cost of a competent and detailed financial-planning team specializing in tax planning. For most of our clients, the tax planning we provide can possibly save them $100,000 or more in taxes over their lifetime. For some, correctly implementing the strategies we advise could even result in tax savings worth millions.

Reducing Lifetime Taxes

Reducing taxes is our primary goal when doing tax planning. Sometimes, this requires our clients to pay more taxes now. An unusual thought, but remember, we have a long-term plan to pay Uncle Sam the least *over a lifetime*.

Our goal is not to pay the least every year, especially when we have times like we're seeing right now, where tax rates are lower than they might be in the future. It might make sense to prepay your taxes now rather than later.

Required Minimum Distribution Planning

Required minimum distributions (RMDs) are when the government forces you to withdraw money from your tax-deferred investments. This is required when you turn seventy-three (if you were born in 1960 or later, this is now seventy-five for you).

I always joke with people and ask, "Is it ever a good thing when the government forces us to do something?" It's usually not a good thing for most Americans.

The other concern with RMDs is the older you get, the more money the government requires you to take out from these accounts. You've probably heard this referred to as a "retirement tax time bomb." It's up to you to plan for this time bomb. Your RMDs may land you in a higher tax bracket or force you to make your withdrawals in the future at higher tax rates (assuming that tax rates increase, as most expect).

There are many tax-planning strategies you can start today that will reduce this burden on your retirement. But when you're not proactive, you're trusting the government to decide what tax rate applies and how much is taken out of your life savings. Do you think the IRS will make your taxes higher or lower in the future?

Roth Conversions

Roth conversions are one of the most popular tax-planning strategies today. We do Roth conversions for the majority of our clients each year.

A Roth conversion takes money from the tax-deferred investments we've been talking about and transitions them to tax-free investments (like a Roth IRA). What is required to do a Roth conversion? Pay taxes, of course. No one likes paying taxes, but would you rather pay the taxes now at a lower rate or later at a higher rate?

When considering Roth conversions, we ask two questions: 1) Should we do a Roth conversion? and 2) How much should we convert?

Roth conversions are not for everyone. They are typically for those who have more saved in their tax-deferred bucket (we usually see it makes a lot of sense for those who have $1 million or more saved) and/or have a pension. If we expect their RMD, pension, and Social Security benefit will force them into a similar or higher tax bracket during retirement, then this could be a strategy to reduce taxes over their retirement. Additionally, for those who anticipate future tax rate increases, a Roth conversion can be even more valuable.

How much to convert gets tricky. This is where the tax software, calculators, and reports come into play. It all comes down to ensuring you pay the lowest tax rate possible on your tax-deferred investment. The choice of how much to convert to a Roth is not simply a matter of tax brackets; other variables such as Medicare premiums, Social Security tax, net investment income tax, alternative minimum tax, and other phase-outs mentioned above will factor into the decision. It takes work to see where you are now and where you are expected to be in the future to make the best decision. Converting too much can lead to overpaying in taxes by pushing yourself into higher tax situations unnecessarily. Converting too little can lead to not taking advantage of lower tax rates and leaving money on the table. It takes a specific process and understanding to find that sweet spot when deciding how much to convert.

Charitable Planning

For our charitable-minded clients, the charitable planning area of tax planning is essential. We never encourage clients to give to charities merely for tax benefits, but we always ensure those giving to charities do so with the most tax efficiency.

There are simple and complex strategies for giving to charities. If you're giving $5,000 or more a year to charities and have no particular strategy in place, I would encourage you to get help. You may be leaving money on the table—money that could be given to your charities or saved in your pocket.

For our clients who give a significant amount of money to charity, we don't want them to give out of their pocket; we want them to implement strategies like a donor-advised fund (DAF) or a qualified charitable distribution (QCD).

Tax Prep

We feel the collaboration between our CPAs and CERTI-FIED FINANCIAL PLANNER® professionals is incredibly important for our clients, to ensure nothing is missed. This has been a big gap we have seen.

Many advisors tell people, "You need to find a CPA to help you with tax planning." But then the CPA tells them, "I only do tax prep, not tax planning." CPAs look backward and are reactive. They're not looking forward and being proactive like those of us who specialize in tax planning. Being proactive means working with a tax planning expert now on a long-term plan for your future income and taxes on it.

We feel this is something that should be done in-house so both professionals are working together. This is why we have a CPA team to make the best decisions for our clients when filing their taxes from January to April. Our team then analyzes our clients' tax returns every year. We will make sure there are no obvious or hidden mistakes, we'll determine if we made the right decisions in the prior year, and we'll better plan for what we can expect things to look like in the year ahead.

If your advisor isn't looking at your tax return every year, then you're likely not getting the tax planning help you need for lifetime tax reduction. It may be that your advisor doesn't specialize in this pillar of planning. We see this situation often—people paying a full price but missing one of the most important pillars in their retirement plan.

Conclusion

I encourage you to get advanced help with your tax planning and to act on it. Our firm has a list of over one hundred tax-saving strategies we use with our clients every year. Many people don't maximize their tax planning because they don't know or understand how to do so.

This chapter gave you an initial taste of the importance of tax planning, and you can read my book *I Hate Taxes* for

a more complete dive into tax planning and to get an understanding of some of those hundred tax-saving strategies I mentioned.

Let's move on to Pillar 2: Investment Planning.

Chapter 2

Pillar 2: Investment Planning

The biggest concern we hear when it comes to investment planning in retirement is this: I do not want to worry about checking the market every day or researching every investment I choose. Many are worried about missing opportunities by taking on too much risk or too little. Others are worried about deciding how to follow market trends and are concerned about making emotional decisions with their life savings. Let's break down these concerns.

Once you're in or near retirement, you may want to change your investing strategy. It may be time to come down the mountain into the "distribution phase."

Have you heard the saying "What got you here won't get you there"? This effectively communicates the idea of having an investment plan when in or near retirement. Think of investment planning like a football game. You've done the work to save (accumulate) a significant amount for your retirement, which puts you on your opponent's twenty-yard line on fourth down, winning by seven points, with only two minutes left in the game. You have options. You can kick a field goal or go for it in an attempt to beat your opponent by more points. You've already won the game. Don't make a mistake that costs you. It's the same thing when it comes to your investment plan. Do you want to take on more risk than you need? Or do you just need a reasonable rate of return that will keep up with inflation so you will not

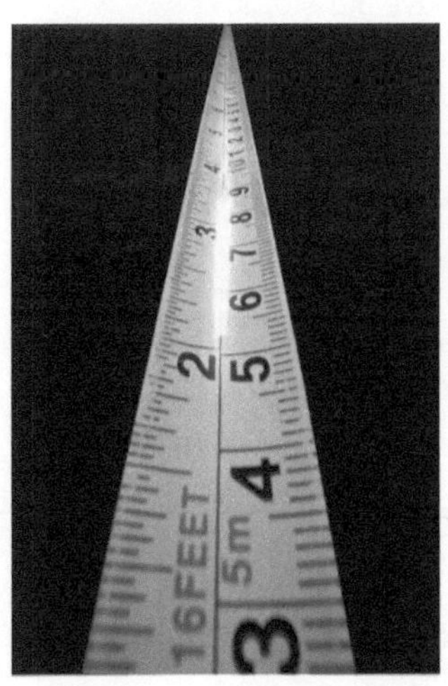

outlive your money? Picture a tape measure extended to ninety inches as a representation of your potential life expectancy. Whatever your current age, you'll see how long you have to plan for so you don't run out of money before you run out of life. When you're twenty-five years old, you have a long way to go on that tape measure until you see the ninety marker and before you have to start taking from your investments. Is it okay to invest more aggressively and for growth right now? Of course it is. At twenty- five you have enough time to make back a market downturn; you have an opportunity when the market goes down.

But when you're farther along that tape measure, say closer to sixty and in the retirement or "distribution phase" (withdrawing money from one or more of your accounts), do you have enough time to make up for a market downturn? How would it feel to spend your retirement wondering if you'll have enough to live on?

Now, understand that this will depend on your risk level, income needs, investment balances, and whether you have a pension or not. Many of our clients can take as much risk as they want or as little risk as possible because they have done a great job saving and/or have pensions.

The Buckets

In or near retirement, you need a rock-solid investment plan that protects and grows your life savings. What does an investment plan look like? We like to refer to two types of buckets: the protection bucket and the growth bucket. This is how we communicate with our clients to simplify the complex topic of investment planning.

Retirement Income Plan

First, you must understand the investment concept that *risk equals return*. The more risk you take (more chance of loss), typically the more return (growth of your investment) you can expect to receive over time. A twenty-five-year-old can expect more return since they'll likely take more risk. A sixty-year-old, however, may want to trade less return for more protection and less chance of loss.

We always ask potential clients about where they sit on a risk scale of zero to one hundred. Zero is an investment with no risk, but with a 3–5 percent return on average, and one hundred is an investment in everything in the stock market where it could do plus 20 percent or minus 20 percent, but usually does more than 3–5 percent over time. Most of our clients answer around forty to sixty. We all want the highest return on our money every year, but that isn't always practical for someone who is risk averse.

I know what you're thinking. "Well, Joe, it would be nice to have an investment that gives me a guaranteed 50 percent return each year with no risk." Unfortunately, that doesn't exist.

I tell people all the time there is no perfect investment. And if anyone tries to sell you on a financial product or investment that's all sunshine and rainbows, you should probably run away. Every investment has pros and cons. What's good for some people might be bad for others. Make sure you have a financial plan that serves your purpose for your money, respects your risk tolerance, and positions your investments in the best way to meet your goals when you need the money.

We work with families who have 90 percent of their money in the growth bucket. They don't plan to touch the money, and maybe they want to leave the biggest inheritance possible to their children. These families are fine with taking risks. They understand that, with a diversified investment plan, what goes down typically comes back up.

We also work with families who have 90 percent of their money in the protection bucket. They see no reason for taking risks; they have enough money and don't need 10 percent or more return every year. They want to keep up with inflation and protect their principal so they don't lose money. Typically, money was tight for them while growing up, and they learned that money equals security. To have the peace of mind they need with their hard-earned life savings, they want to make sure it's there for them.

Whichever bucket you prefer, there is no wrong answer as long as your goals can be met. Everyone's situation is different, and you need the right allocation for you, your goals, and your plan.

Protection Bucket

The protection bucket is made up of investments where a decline in the stock market won't cause you to lose your principal. As a result, this bucket may not return as much money as the growth bucket. Our goal with the protection bucket is to get enough return to keep up with inflation.

The "best" investment for the protection bucket will change over time. Which investment is best here depends on interest rates and the vehicles available in the marketplace. Don't forget, your investment decisions depend on your goals and your time horizon for needing your money. We have a plethora of different options for our clients to choose from.

The types of investments that could be used in the protection bucket include bank accounts, money market accounts, treasuries, annuities, and certificates of deposits (CDs). All of these options have pros and cons, so you must do your due diligence on what is best for you.

Growth Bucket

Think of the growth bucket as nearly the opposite of the protection bucket. In the growth bucket, we're looking to see more return than the protection bucket. Most people have their money invested in typical stocks and bonds, the "60/40" portfolio. Let's break that down to see how that has done over time. In our opinion, today's world offers better ways to structure a 60/40 portfolio to seek more growth and less risk. If your investments are structured this way, your money is at risk. I say that because bonds aren't fully protected. Most people think of bonds as protection for their portfolio, but that's not entirely true. Bonds have had losses at times. Think back to when an aggregate bond index (vested benefit obligation) was down almost 20 percent from the high on August 7, 2020, to October 20, 2022.

Source: Yahoo! Finance

This means that over a two-year period, if you had $500,000 in BND in your IRA or 401(k), you would have lost $100,000 of what you thought was protected money. How would you feel? Many of our clients aren't comfortable taking that amount of risk and would rather have something protected and predictable. We can reduce the amount of risk in our clients' portfolios while still seeking bond-like returns, if not better, over time.

We don't recommend high-risk investments in the growth bucket. Instead, we prefer a diversified portfolio (not having all your eggs in one basket). This means a portfolio which consists of many individual stocks and low cost exchange-traded funds (ETFs)/index funds (investments where you can invest in hundreds of stocks with one investment). Such a diversified portfolio might include investing in large and small companies, US and international companies, value and growth companies, and technology/healthcare/real estate sectors. We would recommend investing in hundreds of companies to plan for worst-case scenarios.

For example, let's say a stock goes to zero. If you had all your retirement savings in one stock, you could lose everything. If you invest in over a hundred companies in addition to that stock, you won't see a significant loss in your investment unless there's a depression and everything in the market loses value. (But we're all in trouble if everything in the market loses value.)

Blending the Buckets

Why are the buckets important? The protection bucket is for the portion of your wealth that you invest more conservatively, or in less risky instruments (but that still earn some profit). The growth bucket allows you to take more risks and hopefully earn greater profits. You need both—to grow your hard-earned money and to beat future inflation—but how do we do that so that you are still comfortable with the allocations? As mentioned, it depends on factors such as your risk level, income needs, investment balances, and whether you have a pension or not. I'll share a few real-life examples.

One of the families we work with has a pension worth $50,000 per year, Social Security equal to $60,000 per year, and $1.2 million saved. They only need an annual income of $80,000 to live on, so we decided to allocate only $200,000 toward the protection bucket. The reason is that they wanted to seek a higher return, knowing their pension was considered part of their protection bucket. They wanted to have enough protection to cover income for emergency expenses that could arise, or for spontaneous things they would decide to spend money on. As we have mentioned, to add a twist to this, they also could have taken on zero risk if they wanted to, since their pension and Social Security covered their income, as they do not need double-digit returns to ensure they have enough investments to live on.

Another family we work with has no pension, $70,000 of Social Security, and $5 million saved. They need $150,000 per year in income to live on. They are worried about the sequence of returns risk (we will discuss this in the next chapter), so we decided to put $800,000 in the protection bucket to ensure they had income for at least ten years if the growth bucket was down. They could have allocated $400,000 to cover five years of income, as it is unlikely the growth bucket would remain down for five consecutive years, but chose to play it safe instead of seeking higher returns (another family we serve in a similar situation opted for a more growth-oriented approach). Now, remember, a 60/40 portfolio would have encouraged them to have $2 million in the protection bucket. That could represent a significant missed growth opportunity over time.

As you can see, there are many ways to look at investment allocation. That is why it is crucial to review your specific situation first before making a decision. Watch out for only following cookie-cutter approaches like the "60/40" portfolio.

Eliminating Unnecessary Fees

I believe that fees are only an issue in the absence of perceived value—and value is perceived differently by different people.

Let me illustrate with an example. Let's say you need to buy a car. You have your choice of two: a brand-new Cadillac or an older beat-up car. For the same amount of money, say $10,000, you could buy either one. What would you do? My guess is you would opt for the brand-new car.

This is what I am talking about with value when it comes to paying for financial advice. Some investment management firms do one of the five pillars, but charge a full price. That's what I would call the older beat-up car. There are also comprehensive retirement planning firms that do the right thing for the client—five out of the five pillars—for the same price. That's what I call the brand-new Cadillac.

We strive to prevent our clients from paying unnecessary fees and ensuring they get the most value for what they pay. We see people who come to us with all in fees of 2–3 percent or more. High fees to that extent will eat into your returns over time.

For our clients, as mentioned previously, we look to use low-cost investments like stocks/index funds/ETFs.

There are many types of fees we'll want to make sure are appropriate. One of these is *internal expenses*. You need to be aware of internal expenses that could be added to your advisor's management fee. Go onto Morningstar and type in your fund's ticker symbol, and you'll see the internal expense of what you're invested in. If your financial planner hasn't told you, consider it a "hidden fee." Stocks have no internal expenses, and index funds/ETFs ordinarily have low internal-expense fees.

We see many people with mutual funds, which have higher fees. Mutual funds aren't bad investments, but most don't outperform a well-diversified portfolio over time. This means you're paying an added cost on top of an advisor's fee for potentially no reason. One thing I like about mutual funds is that they require an active investment approach instead of sitting back. Your financial-planning firm should be actively managing your investments as part of your management fee, not as an added cost. We reduce fees for our clients because we do all investing in-house.

On the protection side of your plan, there are options that don't charge you fees. For example, if you put money in a bank-related product or insurance company, you may not have any direct fees coming out of your return. Think of a CD. If a CD gives you a 3 percent return on your money, then you get a full 3 percent return. No fees come out of that.

Be aware of other fees like trading costs, sales charges, and platform fees. Industry expert Michael Kitces did a study on the average all-in cost of financial advisors and found that the average cost was approximately 1.5 percent for those with $1–2 million of investable assets.[1] We believe families should be paying less than that to get retirement planning guidance for all 5 Pillars.

Make sure you're aware of the total costs when you invest. Some advisors or investment companies can be sneaky. I've seen firms charge a 1 percent management fee but then have a company helping them with the investments that charge 0.5 percent on top of that. There still may be internal expenses as well. And remember to make sure that you are getting all five pillars included in your fee. If you are only getting one out of the five pillars but paying a full price, you may want to ask for a discount or find another retirement planning firm to ensure you get the ongoing value you deserve.

---

1   Michael Kitces, "Financial Advisor Fees Comparison – All-In Costs For The Typical Financial Advisor?" Kitces.com, July 31, 2017, https://www.kitces.com/blog/ independent-financial-advisor-fees-comparison-typical-aum-wealth-management-fee/.

Professional Investment Management

When it comes to investment management, we don't recommend throwing darts when deciding which investments and funds to invest in.

Our firm uses an in-depth and calculated process to decide which investments to suggest to our clients. We also try to follow and take advantage of market trends, which could allow us to overweight a particular part of the market if we expect more upside there.

In my opinion, investing on your own as a do-it-yourself project isn't a promising idea. Imagine meeting with an advisor who has one client, no credentials, and admits that all of their investment choices are inescapably emotional. They have no thorough research or reasoning for investing the way they do. Would you trust this advisor with all of your retirement accounts? But that is exactly what you are doing if you are a DIY investor. There are too many factors to evaluate, and making the wrong investment choices could cause you to have significant loss or take on more risk than you need.

Our approach analyzes the financials of every company and fund when deciding what to invest in and what not to. We review balance sheets, cash flow, profit margins, return on capital, and other financial data that give us a feel for what we might invest in. This is something the average investor doesn't consider. We can't time the market, but by following market trends, we can position our clients' retirement savings much better than throwing darts and hoping the investments do well.

We also recommend making sure the financial planning team you work with uses the help of a Certified Financial Analyst (CFA) when making investment decisions on your portfolio. The CFA credential is the gold star credential in the investment space.

Conclusion

Do you have a plan or a portfolio? A portfolio is a junk drawer of different investments that don't necessarily work together or have a specific purpose. A plan is everything we mentioned above to ensure you're not taking on more risk than you need to while trying to ensure you see enough growth to keep up with inflation. Many people we talk to only have a portfolio. In retirement, a plan is far more comforting.

The next pillar of our strategy is Pillar 3: Income Planning. This is where we decide how to structure your plan and choose investments for retirement income—to get you that "retirement paycheck."

Chapter 3

Pillar 3: Income Planning

The income planning pillar answers the following questions:

- Which accounts should you take from (Roth accounts, traditional accounts, or taxable accounts), and what is the tax impact?

- Which investment buckets (protection or growth) should you pull from?

- How do you avoid market downturns to ensure you don't run out of money?

- When should you take Social Security?

People who meet with us often ask, "How are we going to plan to get a paycheck for life once we stop working?" Now it's time for them to create their own paycheck. For most people, this is something different from anything they have ever done before.

Your retirement years are much more complex than your working years. Retirement takes much more *intentional* planning. Your employer is no longer responsible for providing you with an income, so you must do this yourself in retirement.

Without a paycheck coming in, you must decide when to take Social Security. You must decide which investments and which accounts you'll take out from and when. Make a plan so that you get a paycheck for life—that's how you'll reduce or eliminate the common concern retirees have of running out of money.

If done incorrectly, your income planning may not maximize the amount of juice you can squeeze out of your lifetime of earnings. If you've accumulated a significant retirement nest egg, you may not need to save more. I like to say, "You may not need more money; you may need a better plan." Do the necessary income planning so you know where and how to get that retirement paycheck.

Income planning is a bigger concern than it ever has been because people are now living a retirement that lasts twenty to thirty years. We call this longevity risk.

In 1900, the average life expectancy of a newborn was 32 years. Fast-forward half a century to 1950, and life expectancy was 58. Now our average life expectancy in the United States is 74.8 years for men and 80.2 years for women.[2]

If you want to get your heart racing, look at the increase in lifespan beyond age 100. There were 89,739 centenarians in 2021, or about two centenarians per 10,000 population in the US, which is nearly double the rate from twenty years prior (2001).[3] What if that number again doubles in the coming twenty years? Well, guess what? It won't. It's projected to increase *sixfold* to 589,000 centenarians by 2060.[4]

Will you be one of the "new" centenarians? You just don't know. But you can plan for it. That's the lesson here: We must plan for living much longer than we ever have.

How can you plan to get income for life? First, you must consider Social Security. Social Security covers about 40 percent of a person's income in retirement, on average.[5, 6] You must find a way to get the other 60 percent. How are you going to do that? Many of our clients have pensions to cover

---

2   Saloni Dattani, Lucas Rodés-Guirao, Hannah Ritchie, Esteban Ortiz-Ospina, and Max Roser, "Life Expectancy," Our World in Data, 2023, https://ourworldindata.org/life-expectancy; "Life Expectancy," National Center for Health Statistics, Centers for Disease Control and Prevention, last reviewed May 2, 2024, https://www.cdc.gov/nchs/fastats/life-expectancy.htm.

3   Thomas Perls, "A Human Model of Exceptional Longevity and Aging Well," Centenarian Statistics, Boston University Medical Campus, updated January 1, 2023, https://www.bumc.bu.edu/centenarian/statistics/.

4   Veera Kerhonen, "Number of people aged 100 and over (centenarians) in the United States from 2016 to 2060," Society/Demographics, Statista, February 2, 2024, https://www.statista.com/statistics/996619/number-centenarians-us/.

5   "Retirement Benefits," Social Security Administration, 2024, https://www.ssa.gov/pubs/EN-05-10035.pdf. Accessed January 4, 2024.

6   "Fact Sheet," Social Security Administration, https://www.ssa.gov/news/press/factsheets/basicfact-alt.pdf. Accessed January 4, 2024.

all or a portion of that gap, but most people would answer, "Through the investments we've saved up over the years."

Now let's talk about taking that big bag of money and turning it into an income stream. That process takes us back to our protection and growth buckets.

The Buckets, Again

When building income plans for our clients, we like to structure our investments by having two buckets, protection and growth, as we discussed in the last chapter.

Over the next ten years, we could plan to take income from the protection bucket. We need to ensure that money is protected to avoid the *sequence of returns risk*—as we'll discuss in the following section—or the risk of taking money from our investments when the market is down.

If the market is down when you're withdrawing money from your investments, we refer to that as a *double loss*. One loss because the market is down, and another loss when you reduce your total wealth by spending it year after year for income in retirement. After two losses to your nest egg, you need to know how long it will take to come back, and if you have the time to wait in retirement for it to come back.

The protection bucket is so important for your first ten years of income. Now, we could hold more or less than ten years in the protection bucket. It is a simple rule of thumb, and it depends on the client's risk tolerance and situation. Ten years can be a good rule of thumb if you want to play it safe, considering that over the last fifty years, a diversified portfolio has never been down over a ten-year period.[7] If the market goes down, you'll have enough money in your protection bucket to "buy you time in the market"; in other words, you'll be able to weather a downturn while you wait for the market to come back. Waiting also allows you to seek growth more comfortably in the growth bucket, which should allow you to outpace inflation over the years and continue to grow your nest egg.

Sequence of Returns Risk

$1,000,000 in retirement assets

Followed a broad market index fund and withdrew 4 percent per year, increasing 3 percent per year for inflation

The Smith Family

Retirement Year: 1996

Total Withdrawals:
$1,377,065

Ending Account Balance:
$2,111,556

The Johnson Family

Retirement Year: 1999

Total Withdrawals:
$1,147,066

Ending Account Balance:
$148,000

Johnson Family has
$1,963,556
less than the Smith Family!

---

7   "IFA Index Portfolio 100," Index Fund Advisors, https://www.ifa.com/portfolios/100. Accessed April 3, 2024.

Sequence of Returns Risk

What exactly is sequence of returns risk? The risk that market declines in the early years of your retirement, paired with your ongoing withdrawals, could deplete your finances sooner than you want, thereby significantly reducing the longevity of your portfolio. What does that mean in plain English? You live longer than your money does.

Again, we see many people who are preparing for or in retirement take on too much risk. They haven't made the transition to start to protect their wealth. They're still hanging out on the accumulation side of the mountain.

Let me show you the impact of not protecting your investments if the market goes down during the early years of your retirement. The Smith family and the Johnson family have the same retirement situation, except for one difference—the year they retire. They each have $1 million invested in the stock market and have withdrawn 4 percent from their investment each year, with an assumed 3 percent inflation rate. (See the following image.)

The Smiths retired in 1996. What happened in 1996? The dot-com boom. They happily saw great growth in their investments early in retirement. The Johnsons retired in 1999. What happened in 1999? The dot-com bust, and the market went down. The Johnsons unhappily saw a great decline in their investments early in retirement.

The Johnsons didn't see the growth of the stock market early in their retirement and instead were met with the double loss concept (stock market down plus withdrawing 4 percent per year from their investments). They never had enough time to make it back up. Because of the timing of their retirements and the state of the stock market—the sequence of returns for each of them—the Smiths ended up with nearly $2 million more than the Johnsons.

Sequence of Returns Risk

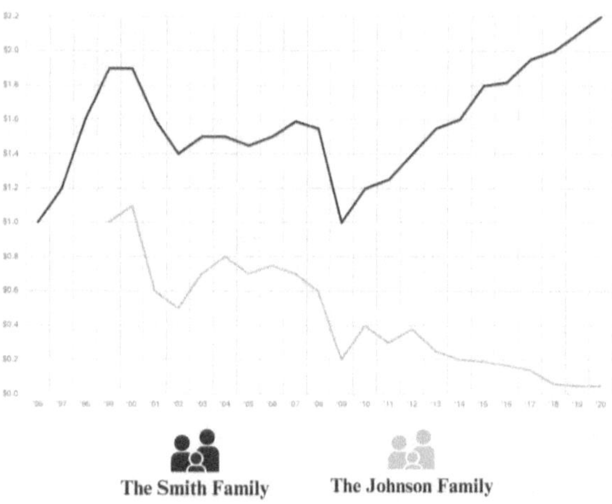

The previous chart shows how the two retirements played out. As you can see, when the Smiths hit the dot-com bust, they had nearly $1.9 million and had taken out income for the last four years. So even through the market crash, they still had over $1.4 million—more than they started with and already six years into retirement. Not much to worry about for them so far. But what about 2008? We all remember how badly the stock market dropped. Well, they still have $1 million, and they're over ten years into retirement. Taking all the income they needed over the years, the Smiths still have more than they started with. That's a good place to be.

As for the Johnsons, they saw a market downturn early in their retirement. Their $1 million turned into $500,000 within three years (because of the double loss). Three years into retirement and they have nearly half of what they started with. The market always comes back, you say? Yes, but do they have the time for it to come back? As you can see, after the second bear market, the Johnsons were left with less than $200,000 in their investments. How long will that last them? How long will they live? Poor timing can lead to these concerns.

How do we plan for sequence of returns risk? By having a plan. In the bucket approach, we provide a plan so you can enjoy retirement and not be concerned about taking out money when the market is down.

Planning for Inflation

Our goal is to always inflation-proof our clients' retirement plans. This means we must get enough growth on our clients' income to keep up with inflation. Historically, inflation has been around 3 percent. So, if you need $5,000 a month to live on today, in twenty years you'll need $10,000 a month to live the same lifestyle.

Inflation mostly impacts retirees because you go from making an income to no longer working and living on a fixed income. You need to plan accordingly. If you don't plan correctly, you may have to work longer.

The good news is, if you plan correctly and implement a retirement income plan like we're talking about, then you'll be able to statistically increase your chances of success and live the retirement you dream of.

We plan for inflation by positioning your investments in the correct way—the bucket concept we've been discussing. For those first ten years of retirement, you pull your income from the protection bucket. That gives you ten years' time in the market to get growth for your growth bucket investments. We would also suggest seeking investments in the protection bucket that will outpace or keep up with inflation.

Social Security Planning

Everyone says that Social Security is running out, but why do they say that? Because Social Security is in trouble.

Let's look into the numbers. Ten thousand baby boomers turn sixty-five every day, as has been the case for the last ten years and will be for ten more.[8] Large numbers of Americans are entering the system and now need their Social Security benefit. You might be one of them. Plus, not as many people are paying into Social Security today. Back in 1935 there were over forty workers to one retiree, and now that ratio is down to three to one.[9] Social Security also wasn't designed to be paid out for twenty-plus years. As more people (the above-mentioned boomers) need Social Security, these numbers lead to concerns.

I don't think Social Security will run out for the baby boomer generation. Our legislators can make a multitude of changes to keep it in place. The last time the federal government "saved" Social Security was in 1983. That seems like a long time ago, but the US Congress can do it again.[10] How? They changed the retirement age, and they can do it again. Now Social Security can be taxable when you take your benefit (which wasn't always the case), and they could give fewer cost-of-living increases over time that may not fully keep up with inflation.

---

8   Hunter Kuffel, "What Retiring Baby Boomers Mean for the Economy," Smart Asset, updated September 8, 2023, https://smartasset.com/retirement/baby-boomers-retiring.

9   "Fact Sheet."

10   Paul C. Light, "The Crisis Last Time: Social Security Reform," Brookings, March 5, 2005, https://www.brookings.edu/articles/the-crisis-last-time-social-security-reform/.

As mentioned earlier, on average the Social Security benefit will account for 40 percent of a retiree's income in retirement. So let's plan on Social Security being there for you.

Now that you understand more about Social Security, you'll want to know the best time to start collecting. The magical answer is "It depends." I've considered not using that phrase anymore. I was at an event talking about Social Security, and a man came up to me after and told me, "I loved the event, Joe, but you need to stop saying 'depends'; you're talking to a bunch of old folks." Hopefully, that made you laugh after all the doom and gloom about the current state of Social Security. But seriously, when to take your benefits depends on many factors.

One of the most important factors is health, or in other words, how long are you going to live? I'm often quoted as saying, "Tell me when you're going to die, and I'll tell you the best time to take Social Security." Obviously, a joke, but it rings true. If you die early, waiting to take Social Security could be a mistake. If you live a long time, taking it early could lead to less total money received from Social Security over the years and a much lower benefit in your later years.

I know the analytically minded reading this book are wondering, "How long do I need to live for it to make sense to take Social Security at seventy versus taking it at sixty-two?" Or, in simpler terms, how long will it take to go eight years without Social Security for the bigger benefit at age seventy to pay off?

Any time between age eighty to eighty-three is the breakeven of when it makes sense to take your benefit at seventy. With life expectancy right around there, it can be tough to decide what's best to do. And that's why we look at other factors:

Money needs. If you need the money now, you may want to take your benefit right away.

Survivor planning. Are you worried about ensuring your spouse is left with the most Social Security benefit possible if you pass? Taking Social Security at seventy could provide your spouse with the highest benefit when you pass because the surviving spouse is left with the higher of the two Social Security benefits.

Spousal benefit. The spousal benefit is for a spouse who hasn't earned as much Social Security or hasn't worked long enough to be entitled to a Social Security benefit. Under the spousal benefit, the lower-earning spouse can elect half of their spouse's benefit (if theirs is less than half).

Taxes. Some people want to maximize their Social Security benefits while also being tax smart. They delay their Social Security and withdraw the income they need from their tax-deferred investments while they wait. Why? Because they'll likely be in a lower bracket without Social Security, and they won't be required to take out as much in the future, which could significantly increase their income if they continue to wait to take out from those accounts. In other words, taking Social Security at seventy could lead to more tax planning and the highest amount. This could also allow you to avoid the infamous Social Security "tax torpedo," which can happen when you take out too much money from your investments and force your Social Security to be fully taxable, and you end up paying a 40–50 percent all-in tax rate.

I wrote an article called "Will You Pay Higher Taxes in Retirement?" about the tax torpedo and ways to pay less tax. Check it out; you can find it featured on Kiplinger.com.[11]

Pension Planning

One of our specialties is planning for those with pensions. We get lots of clients who come from our YouTube channel all across the country because of this focus. These are people who are former military or federal employees, state employees, firefighters, police officers, teachers, etc.

We love helping these people, as they are typically the prominent hardworking Midwestern Millionaires we talk about. Pension planning is complex. Those with pensions are forced to make lots of decisions on their pension when

---

11   Joe F. Schmitz Jr., "Will You Pay Higher Taxes in Retirement?", Kiplinger, May 10, 2023, https://www.kiplinger.com/retirement/will-you-pay-higher-taxes-in-retirement.

they retire: Should they take a lump sum or partial lump sum? Should they take a 100% survivorship option, 50% survivorship option, or none at all? Are they okay with none at all, or would they be better off to get a life insurance policy to replace the survivor pension?

We have software and strategies to help our clients maximize these decisions. These are one-time decisions, and a single bad decision here can lead to less in retirement.

Pension planning also involves tax planning with pensions. Many of our clients with pensions complain about the amount of taxes they are paying in retirement. I use the word "complain" loosely, as this is a great problem to have. Proper proactive planning with a pension with tax strategies we have discussed can make a world of difference on the overall tax they will pay in their lifetime.

If you find yourself with a pension and consider yourself that "Midwestern Millionaire" we have talked about, then you may want to check out my book titled *The 2% Club*. This book is about pension planning for those with $1 million or more saved. I came up with the title from the concept that nowadays, fewer than 20 percent of people have a pension, and fewer than 10 percent of people have saved $1 million or more. When you combine those two percentages, you are left with only 2 percent of the population in this situation. Their planning will require more advanced strategies to ensure they plan not only for a high income but also for a high net worth. This is a niche we specialize in serving.

Tax-Efficient Withdrawal Strategy

Deciding where to take income from your investments and understanding the tax impact can be difficult, as we have already mentioned. Should you take the income you need in retirement from your IRA/401k, where it is fully taxed? Should you take it from your nonqualified accounts, which are taxed at capital gains on any of the growth you have seen? Or should you take it out from your Roth accounts, which are tax free? These are not easy questions to answer. However, when a solution is successfully implemented, you can efficiently take out thousands of dollars more each year due to the tax savings you can realize. It is important to understand how the standard deduction plays a part here, along with the taxation of Social Security and the calculation of Medicare premiums, tax brackets, and projected future income. This is something we take very seriously with our clients to ensure that the income they get is maximized.

Conclusion

A proactive retirement income plan like this requires constant diligence to make consistent changes. But not change for the sake of change. You take advantage of opportunities as they arise throughout your retirement.

Interconnected to the pillars of tax planning, investment planning, and income planning is your healthcare situation. Healthcare costs can decimate your wealth—which is why having a plan is so important. The next chapter covers Pillar 4: Healthcare Planning.

Chapter 4

Pillar 4: Healthcare Planning

Healthcare costs are a considerable risk in retirement since the majority of us will have health concerns in our retirement years.

Fidelity did a study claiming that the average retiree will spend over $150,000 on healthcare expenses over their lifetime, not including long-term care.[12] For a married couple, that could be over $300,000.

How are we going to plan for this?

Medicare Planning

Let's start with the big Medicare decision you must make at the magical age of sixty-five. We go through a review with our clients to decide what level of supplemental policy they should get in addition to their Medicare Part A and Part B.

---

12   "How to plan for rising health care costs," Fidelity, June 21, 2023, https://www.fidelity.com/viewpoints/personal-finance/plan-for-rising-health-care-costs.

Part A comes at no cost; it's what you've paid for all your life. Part B comes at an additional cost and is means-based, which means the higher your income, the more you must pay.

It's not fair that certain people have to pay more for Medicare Part B. Think about it: Someone wasn't diligent in saving for retirement and didn't work hard to accumulate retirement savings, which means they have a lower income. Someone who made sacrifices to save for retirement and spent more time planning their retirement is penalized by having to pay more for the same Medicare coverage.

Planning for Medicare premiums serves as an excellent example to show you how the pillars are interwoven. Pillars 1 and 3—Tax Planning and Income Planning—are necessary precursors to good Healthcare Planning. We want lower Medicare premiums for our clients, so it is ideal for them to show the IRS a lower income in retirement (income planning and tax planning for moving money to tax-free accounts).

You must be meticulous about taking money out of your investments and closely examining the tax consequences.

Supplemental Medicare Plans

Once you have Part A and B in place, most people need to start looking for a supplemental policy and a stand-alone prescription drug plan. Part A and B may not be adequate for most.

I suggest you work with a Medicare expert who understands the Medicare marketplace. Our clients meet with a

Medicare expert on our team six months before they take their benefit. Together, we shop for the best plan at the best cost while also considering health history and possible medications.

There are hundreds of plans out there, so get expert advice to ensure you make the right decision.

Long-Term Care Planning

As we all know, long-term care is a significant concern for retirees. People are living longer, but not healthier, which means many people may need skilled nursing one day.

Statistics show that 70 percent of retirees will need long-term care at some point in their life. The average long-term care stay for most is around two to five years.[13]

When we talk about long-term care, we're talking about needing help with the activities of daily living. There are six main activities elderly people need to be able to do for themselves (or consider getting care): bathing, dressing, toileting, transferring (getting in and out of bed or a chair), eating, and continence.

You also must consider cognitive impairment, another cause of needing long-term care. Alzheimer's and other forms of dementia are becoming more common, and these conditions can not only prolong the need for long-term care but also require more specialized care, which could be costly.

---

13   "How Much Care Will You Need?," Data from the ACL, Administration for Community Living, an agency of the U.S. Department of Health & Human Services, last modified February 18, 2020, https://acl.gov/ltc/basic-needs/how-much-care-will-you-need.

Long-term care assistance can be provided in many different ways. A nurse could come to your house to assist you, you could go to an assisted living facility with help nearby, or go to a nursing home where you can get consistent help. The type of assistance will depend on your need for help, cost, and comfort.

Because of those ten thousand baby boomers turning sixty-five every day, the need (and cost) for long-term health-care is skyrocketing. Think of it as supply and demand. The fewer nurses and skilled caretakers we have to take care of retirees with long-term care needs, and the more people needing that care, the cost will go up. And it's already high. Consider these statistics from Genworth's annual Cost of Care Survey for 2024:

Annual Cost of Care (USA National, 2024) [14]		
In-Home Care	**Community and Assisted Living**	**Nursing Home Facility**
Homemaker Services: $75,504 Change Since 2023: 10%	Adult Day Healthcare: $26,000 Change Since 2023: 5%	Semi-Private Room: $111,325 Change Since 2023: 7%
Home Health Aide: $77,792 Change Since 2023: 3%	Assisted Living Facility: $70,800 Change Since 2023: 10%	Private Room: $127,750 Change Since 2023: 9%

14   Clark, Ryan. "Genworth and CareScout Release Cost of Care Survey Results for 2024." Genworth Financial, Inc., March 4, 2025. https://investor.genworth.com/news-events/press-releases/detail/982/genworth-and-carescout-release-cost-of-care-survey-results.

What are we going to do to help you prepare for long-term care and its rising costs? There are many ways to plan for long-term care, but here are six of the most common:

Self-insuring. For those with more assets, self-insuring may be more realistic. Self-insuring means you pay from your retirement savings for the care you need. You'll see the pros and cons of the list below to help you decide if you can do more. If you decide to self-insure, structuring your investments appropriately will be even more important to prepare for a big potential bill coming your way. Many of our clients choose this option along with one or two of the options below.

Medicaid. Medicaid planning is a strategy that tends to say, "I'm not going to plan for healthcare; the government can take care of me." Many people plan this way because they may not have the assets to self-insure or to do any of the other strategies we discussed. The good news: The government will provide care for you once you have depleted your assets to a low amount. The bad news: You'll have low assets, which means you may not be able to do anything extra in your retirement except get healthcare from Medicaid. This could mean less money left behind when you pass away.

Trust (estate planning). A Medicaid Asset Protection Trust (MAPT) is a legal document. Creating this trust allows individuals to qualify for Medicaid while protecting their assets from being depleted if long-term care is needed. It is a complex document and must be prepared by a specialist attorney. These trusts are not for everyone, but they can be a unique way to plan for long-term care risk. This strategy moves money out of your estate and into an irrevocable trust. The government can't come after it once the assets outside of the trust are spent down.

Many people think irrevocable means you can't access these assets while you're living. That's right, but if the trust is structured correctly, you still retain access to your funds if needed. Once you pass away, these assets can be transferred to your final beneficiary without Medicaid coming in to take what they feel entitled to.

There are many requirements to meet and to be aware of for the assets in the trust to be eligible, and these rules are ever-changing. We recommend working not only with a financial planning team but also working closely with an estate planning team that specializes in elder law to ensure you are making an educated and informed decision.

When evaluating this trust for our clients, we look at how many assets they have to determine if the cost to create this trust is worth the value they could potentially receive.

Gifting. If you're worried about your money being spent down to be used for care, then one idea is to start gifting now and get the money out of your estate. This strategy is most popular for those wanting to give to a charity or to their kids.

This gifting strategy is similar to the trust strategy we just discussed. The difference is that you don't have to pay to get legal documents drafted. It may not be as official as you can imagine. Like a trust, many requirements must be met, and you should consult with a professional to make sure you're taking the right steps.

Home equity line of credit (or home equity conversion mortgage). Be careful with a home equity line of credit. You need the right situation (a lot of equity in your home) and the right time (a low interest rate) for this strategy to make sense. A home equity line of credit could allow you to take out money when the market is down and not worry about taxes from your investments if you were to plan for long-term care that way.

Insurance. Some people look to insurance for long-term care protection and security. All the strategies mentioned so far have their pros and cons, and planning with insurance is no different.

There are many types of insurance you could use. Long-term care insurance is a way to leverage your money to get more money for the care you're looking for, but it can be costly, and you have to be medically eligible for an insurance company to insure you. The cost of long-term care insurance has soared recently, making it less favorable in my opinion. We use this strategy less often now with our clients than we used to. That could change in the future, so it's important to stay up to date on long-term care planning. If you have a policy that was issued when Long Term Care Insurance was more affordable, then you may have a really good deal. We typically encourage our clients to keep those in place.

A permanent life insurance policy is another way to plan for long-term care. Some life insurance allows you to accelerate the death benefit for long-term care. Life insurance has the advantage of being a Swiss Army™ knife. You could cancel the policy if you don't need long-term care and take the cash value (which could be the amount you paid into the policy or more) to do what you want with it. You also could leave a legacy to your spouse or beneficiaries if you never need it for long-term care when you pass away. That death benefit would also be tax-free. The other advantage of long-term care insurance or life insurance is that the long-term care benefit you use from the policy is tax-free to you.

Annuities are another way to use insurance to plan for long-term care. Annuities can be complex, and there are many options, but some annuities allow you to have protection when you need the money. You don't have to worry about a market downturn, and you can access extra money without a penalty if you need long-term care assistance.

The best way to plan is going to be specific to your financial situation and goals. With our clients, we walk through and evaluate each option with them and help them decide what will be best for their specific situation.

As we discussed, healthcare costs, including out-of-pocket expenses, tend to increase the older we get and also over time with the need rising. We must be prepared and have funds available to pay for anything that may come up. We expect this to happen. And in some years, you may be able to use the high cost of healthcare to write off on your taxes, which can lead to tax-planning opportunities. Working with someone who specializes in retirement planning ensures you're not leaving money on the table.

Planning for Early Retirement

We have clients who decide to retire early. Retiring early in this definition means retiring before age 65. This is something that needs to be planned for, because early retirees lose their health insurance through work and are not yet eligible for Medicare, which doesn't start until age 65. This means they must seek assistance to get health insurance on the open market. There are many options to consider. Our clients get the help of our health insurance specialist who specializes in helping people under the age of sixty-five find the right coverage and plan to fit their needs and budget.

The other important planning items for those retiring early deal with income planning. Early retirees may not be eligible for Social Security or a pension yet; if not, they must derive all of their income from their investments. The early retirement years are also an important time for tax planning: since early retirees no longer have an income from working, it can be an optimal time to take advantage of the lower tax brackets and implement tax savings strategies before other taxes come into play during retirement.

Conclusion

Healthcare can be a big cost and a big risk in retirement. I've personally seen this risk not only in our clients' lives but also in my family's lives. If you know someone who has had health issues in retirement or needed long-term care, then you know the severity of the financial and emotional toll. The best way to overcome healthcare risks is to be proactive and plan.

It's time to wrap up much of what we've discussed, as well as expand on it, because Pillar 5: Estate Planning is coming up next. Last, but not least.

Chapter 5

Pillar 5: Estate Planning

Before I get into the details of a successful estate plan, you must first understand what estate planning means. Estate planning is planning for the end of life. You'll need certain documents in place, you'll possibly need to prepare for the loss of a spouse, and you'll need to be tax smart when transferring wealth (so that Uncle Sam isn't the biggest beneficiary of what you've accumulated).

When it comes to estate planning, you must know your purpose and goals. Only then can you make the right decisions for your wealth now *and* when you're no longer here.

So many people say they need to get an estate plan in place but never do. Everyone age eighteen and up needs an estate plan, but 67 percent of Americans die without one.[15] When should you do it? It should already be done. If it isn't, we encourage you to plan for one as soon as possible. We all know that anything can happen at any time.

We help our clients facilitate estate planning documents (trusts, wills, powers of attorney, living wills, updates to beneficiaries, etc.) and then we take it a step further. Too often people go to an estate planning attorney and pay to get the documents they need, but then they never put them in place. Those documents never get used, and people aren't protected. Our team is involved in every part of our clients' plan to ensure the client is getting what they need and they do not need to go to multiple different professionals to get the job done. Sadly, this isn't always the case. Also, keep in mind most estate planning attorneys can charge $4,000-$5,000 on average to put a full trust and estate planning package in place. Some charge even more. We help facilitate this for our clients to ensure they can save money and extra work.

We are big advocates of this one-stop-shop approach and recommend that those looking to work with a team have it in place to ensure nothing gets missed.

---

15   Lorie Konish, "67% of Americans have no estate plan, survey finds. Here's how to get started on one," *Advice and the Advisor*, CNBC, April 11, 2022, https://www.cnbc.com/2022/04/11/67percent-of-americans-have-no-estate-plan-heres-how-to-get-started-on-one.html.

There are different levels of complexity to consider when it comes to estate planning. Let's start with basic documents, probate, and trusts.

Basic Documents

Financial and healthcare powers of attorney. A financial power of attorney (POA) and a healthcare POA are two documents. Everyone needs them, and they are the most important pair of documents to have. It allows someone to make financial and healthcare decisions for you if you cannot. For instance, if you were in a car accident, traveling abroad, or developed dementia and couldn't make your own decisions, the POA states who can.

Living will. The living will document states your end-of-life healthcare decisions and wishes. It indicates things like stopping (or not) life support or proceeding (or not) with a surgery.

Will, or last will and testament. A will (or last will and testament) includes things listed later in this chapter, but it doesn't avoid probate (other steps will need to be taken to achieve this, which we'll discuss below). A will designates an executor who carries out the provisions of the will. It will include instructions for how the beneficiaries will receive the assets.

Health Insurance Portability and Accountability Act of 1996 (HIPAA). HIPAA is a privacy-protection law.

You must make a written statement to allow someone to be able to talk to a doctor for you. The spouse can't get health-care information without being named. Many people put their kids on this written statement as well.

Transfer on death (TOD). A TOD transfers assets and avoids probate. It is mainly used for houses, rental properties, vehicles, and investment accounts that aren't retirement accounts. We see many people without this designation on their assets which could be a costly mistake.

Payable on death (POD). Very similar to a TOD mentioned above, but a POD is for your bank accounts.

Beneficiaries. Beneficiaries are those who are inheriting the assets. We make sure our clients have the correct beneficiaries on file for their accounts. If there's a mistake or the listed beneficiary dies, the accounts may go to probate. Having beneficiaries on file ensures ease of transfer when you pass away.

How to Avoid Probate

Probate is the legal process following a person's death that deals with their assets and debts. It validates asset distribution to beneficiaries and resolves debt issues. Probate is overseen by the court and ensures the proper transfer of assets.[16]

---

16   Julie Kagan, "Probate: What It Is and How It Works With and Without a Will," Investopedia, updated May14, 2024, https://www.investopedia.com/terms/p/probate.asp

Titling your retirement accounts and insurance policies by beneficiary will ensure they avoid probate. Titling your other assets by TOD or POD as mentioned will also allow those assets to avoid probate.

Avoiding probate is important because the probate process could cost 4–7 percent of an estate that is not prepared for it. Probate is also time consuming and difficult to work through. Most people want to avoid this tedious process. By planning the right way, you can avoid probate.

Do I Need a Trust?

Needing a trust depends on your situation. Some may not need a trust if they have more basic financial situations that can pass by naming beneficiaries and properly titling assets, as discussed. Although, there are some things to consider.

A trust could be good to use under the following scenarios:

- You have a complex situation. If you have multiple rental properties, properties in multiple states, or numerous assets in different places, a trust could make sense.

- You don't trust your beneficiaries. If you want to limit your children on how much they can spend each year and not have access to all the money at once, a trust can structure specific payments every year of the children's lives.

- You want to keep your money in the bloodline.

- You have minor children (under eighteen years). A trust makes sure the children will have detailed plans for using the funds and know who will be there to monitor things.

- You want to avoid probate. This is one of the main reasons estate planning attorneys recommend a trust, but this could be done by proper planning without a trust in most scenarios as mentioned above.

- You are planning for long-term care as mentioned in Chapter 4 with a Medicaid Asset Protection Trust.

- You seek to reduce estate taxes. This may not be a concern right now but could be a concern if the government lowers the estate tax limits. We monitor this continually with many of our clients considering this limit has been less than $1 million in the past and would require you to pay around a 40 percent tax on any amount above the limit.

As an example, residents of our home state of Ohio may not need a trust, since they can designate their assets as "transfer on death" (TOD). However, other states do not accept a TOD designation, meaning that the only way to pass your assets to your loved ones without probate would be to utilize a trust. We have clients all over the country, so this is something that we always look into. Many of our clients get a trust to play it safe and ensure everything is covered.

Survivor Planning

In addition to the estate planning documents discussed above, you'll want to make sure your spouse has additional planning items in place if you were to pass away.

When it comes to survivor planning, people in or near retirement focus on consolidating their assets wherever possible. Instead of having four different 401(k) accounts at different companies, you may look to roll those over to one account in an IRA. You'll make things easier for your beneficiary when you pass away, and they won't have to spend a great deal of time and hassle getting things organized.

Many of our clients work with us to consolidate their assets and have a trusted guide for their spouse when they pass. We work with many couples where one knows everything about their financial situation and the other knows nothing, or next to nothing. They appreciate the comfort that comes from having a trusted and vetted team who will continue with the plan if something happens to the more knowledgeable spouse. If this describes your situation, and you're not working with an advisor, you may want to do so now. Get a plan together and start building that trusted connection if you pass away before your spouse.

Reducing Taxes to Beneficiaries

Back to my favorite topic of taxes. Remember how I said taxes are factored into every pillar? As you can guess, taxes play a big part in leaving a legacy to your beneficiaries.

When you're married and one of you passes away, the surviving spouse is faced with something called the "widow's penalty." You go from "married filing jointly" for the year your spouse passes to "single" the following year. There's a big difference between married filing jointly and single. The tax brackets are nearly cut in half, meaning the surviving spouse could pay nearly double the amount of taxes.

I have a real-life client example to help you understand how severe the widow's penalty can be—and why you must plan for it.

Ralph and Vicky are married. The following chart outlines their incomes. The column on the far left shows their current situation while both are living. As you can see, Ralph has a generous Social Security benefit, and Vicky gets the spousal benefit, which is half of Ralph's. The couple also has RMDs of $60,000. Their current situation has a total tax bill of $10,823.

What happens if Ralph or Vicky passes away and they do not make any changes to their plan? As you can see in the middle, one of the Social Security benefits goes away, and the surviving spouse can keep the higher of the two. The RMD would remain the same since all the accounts would have the spouse as beneficiary. In this scenario, the surviving spouse now has a lower income and must pay higher taxes. This is the widow's penalty in full effect.[17]

The "Widow's Penalty"

How do you avoid such a penalty? By planning for it before it's too late! Using strategies found throughout this book, you must lower your taxable income in the future by

---

17   Joe F. Schmitz Jr., "How Not to Let the 'Widow's Tax Penalty' Blindside You," CPA Practice Advisor, November 6, 2023, https://www.cpapracticeadvisor.com/2023/11/06/how-not-to-let-the-widows-tax-penalty-blindside-you/97300/.

living on tax-free investments so that you're not forced to pay higher taxes in scenarios like this. As you can see on the far right of the preceding image, by integrating a tax-free vehicle like a Roth into the plan, we were able to significantly lower our clients' lifetime tax bill, ensuring they do not overpay in taxes. Or as I like to say, "not tipping Uncle Sam." We allowed them to be in a lower tax bracket by taking tax-free income from the Roth and also provided for more of their Social Security benefit to be tax-free.

The widow's penalty is one of my biggest problems with the tax code. An already vulnerable spouse is put at yet another disadvantage. Not only do they lose out on the Social Security benefits but they also must pay more tax. Plan before it is too late is my advice.

Reducing Taxes to Non-Spouse Beneficiaries

New laws require that beneficiaries must take money out of retirement accounts over a ten-year period under most circumstances when leaving money to, for example, their children.

Why is this notable? People used to be able to stretch these accounts over their lifetime, giving them the flexibility to strategically withdraw the funds and not force them to take a large portion out over a short amount of time. But now, since the money must be taken out over ten years, people could be forced into a higher income bracket, which means Uncle Sam gets more than he used to.

Plan for this. As we mentioned earlier, transferring your accounts to tax-free investments, like a Roth, so your children won't have to worry about paying taxes on these withdrawals over the ten-year period could be a good idea to consider. Life insurance could also be a useful strategy to reduce taxes for your heirs. The death benefit from life insurance is tax-free to your heirs.

Purpose Planning

One of our favorite things to do with those we work with is to help them find more purpose with their money, whether that means spending more or giving more (either now or when they pass away). Many of the "Midwestern Millionaires" we work with are great savers but terrible spenders (as we call it). We have to encourage them to change their mindset at this point in their life, as they cannot take all of this wealth with them when they pass away. We want to see our clients enjoy and see value in what they have worked so hard to accumulate. For some of our clients, that means travelling more. For others, it means retiring early. Some want to give more to kids and grandkids while they are still alive, so they can see the impact of their gifts. Others would like to give to their favorite charities or churches to make an impact in this world bigger than themselves. Whatever that is for our clients, we want to see it get lived out. We do this by having intentional conversations about purpose planning, and also by holding them accountable. Many people do not understand how much they have until we show them how well-off they are—that even if they spend extra money each month, they will still be overly set up for success in retirement. These are exciting conversations and what purpose planning is all about.

Conclusion

Estate planning means you have a plan in place before it's too late. Your loved ones will thank you. Procrastinating can be costly.

Closing Remarks

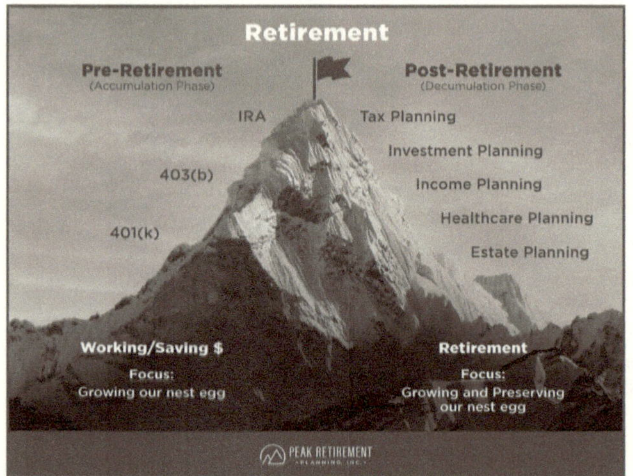

We started the book with this mountain image and will close the book with it as well. Going down the slope post-retirement is much different from going up the mountain during your pre-retirement working years.

During the climbing time, you were thinking, "Grow, grow, grow." Now, during the descent, it's time to think, "Protect, protect, protect."

The goal of our 5 Pillar Approach is to protect the wealth you've worked hard to accumulate. We want you to enjoy it and reap the rewards.

We specifically chose our firm's name, Peak Retirement Planning, Inc., because we help people climb safely down this complex mountain of retirement. This is what we do all day long. *We plan retirements.* We are different from most firms in our industry with our focus and approach. We're the specialists, not general practitioners.

Retirement is the most extended and biggest vacation of your life. We encourage you to prepare and get professional help. If you haven't planned hundreds of retirements before, then you may want to get help from a team who has.

When the 5 pillars of retirement planning are implemented correctly, you can enjoy a wondrous, worry-free retirement.

Imagine how good it will feel to travel when you want, to volunteer where and when you want, and to retire when you want. You'll get to spend time with grandkids and not worry about missing key areas with your life savings. You can rest assured that you're set up to live a successful retirement.

My advice to everyone reading this book is to get professional analysis and planning assistance, whether with us or someone else. Don't go down the mountain of retirement with a blindfold on and no trusted guide. You need someone—a whole team—who knows how to navigate you down the slope and has been there before.

If our team can be of value to your retirement, learn more about us and schedule a session at:

www.PeakRetirementPlanning.com

A SNEAK PREVIEW OF

MIDWESTERN MILLIONAIRE

(1)

THE TRAITS OF A MIDWESTERN MILLIONAIRE

Let me be clear about the Midwestern Millionaire. This isn't about American geography. You don't have to live in the Midwest to be a Midwestern Millionaire. We work with people living all across the country, and many of our clients who live on the East or West Coast and down South meet these criteria and have the same values as Midwesterners.

The following list outlines eight of the key traits we see in the Midwestern Millionaire:

1. Diligent Saver

As mentioned, the Midwestern Millionaire has saved at least $1 million. This is no easy accomplishment, considering all the things life can throw at you over the years. They have done this by being . . .

2. Frugal

Midwestern Millionaires are great savers and the worst spenders. That's how I like to explain it. It is that pair of "money habits" that has allowed them to accumulate their wealth.

They often like saving money on ordinary purchases, and they're content without having the most luxurious items. They're frugal; it's second nature to them. If they find blueberries on sale at the store, they stock up. At the end of this chapter, I'll tell a funny story about blueberries to emphasize this trait, which goes hand-in-hand with . . .

3. Hardworking

Midwestern Millionaires are willing to do whatever it takes, however long it takes. They are conscientious and consistent workers. They put their head down and get things done. My parents are two of the hardest workers I know and couldn't be better examples of Midwestern Millionaires.

My dad taught me that the day isn't over until the job is done. My mom taught me that you must give 100 percent in everything you do, often saying, "How you do anything is how you do everything."

They do everything needed because as Midwestern Millionaires, they . . .

4. Want to Pay Less in Taxes

They believe their hard-earned income and their life savings should be in their pockets and not in Uncle Sam's. They never want to overpay in taxes. Now, they're not against paying taxes, but they only want to pay their fair share and not "tip" Uncle Sam anything extra. They believe the government isn't necessarily the best steward of their taxpaying dollars. They believe in lowering taxes to allow for "We the People" to have more control over the economy, as opposed to giving more to the government and allowing them to control how our money is spent. People with Midwestern values also typically don't believe in handouts; they believe what you get is earned and not given.

The more money you have, the more tax you pay. Midwestern Millionaires know they will pay lots of taxes over their retirement unless they start successfully implementing tax-planning strategies now. They're also . . .

5. Risk-Averse

They want to protect their savings. Midwestern Millionaires are more conservative in their investing approach and want to find investments that are less aggressive and more stable and consistent over time. Yes, they want a return, but they don't want to take on more risk than they need to. They may want to achieve single and doubles now instead of swinging for the fences.

They also want to protect their wealth from health-care bills (they've heard or seen how medical costs can be extremely costly throughout retirement). They strive to ensure that their wealth will transfer to their spouse and children without losing any of that wealth. They don't want to miss anything. This proves they are also . . .

6. Family-Oriented

Family is extremely important to Midwestern Millionaires. I've always been told to take care of those who take care of me. Likewise, many of our clients truly care about making sure their family is taken care of.

Our clients want their spouse to be taken care of when they pass away, and they want their kids and grandkids to have the opportunities and resources that will set them up for success. We can help them build financial plans that prepare for the loss of a spouse and build generational wealth for their families in the future.

One way we do this is through advanced tax planning. Midwestern Millionaires love learning about and imple-menting strategies that will ensure their family gets more of their wealth than Uncle Sam. We also do smart estate planning using strategies that allow the smooth transfer of assets to the next generation. We see that as not only having estate documents (which are extremely important) but also by having a rock-solid estate plan that incorporates advanced tax planning and purpose.

Midwestern Millionaires know they are blessed with wealth, but they remain . . .

7. Humble

You would never know the Midwestern Millionaire is a millionaire and has had extreme success over their lifetime. They don't always drive a flashy car or live in the biggest house. They don't participate in the latest fashion trends or spend thousands of dollars on clothing. One of our clients wears the same shirt nearly every time we see him (yes, it's washed). It's an Old Navy shirt from twenty years ago with an American flag on it. Is he still wearing it because he can't afford a new shirt? No, he wears it because he is content with what he has and is not trying to impress others with new fancy clothing. He even says, "They don't make shirts like they used to." He has bought a product of quality from a manufacturer he believes shares his own commitment to being . . .

8. Trusting and Trustworthy

Because the needed planning is so complex, many Midwestern Millionaires work with a team as they prepare for retirement and work through retirement. This means they trust a team to help manage what they have worked so hard to accumulate for the last forty years. That kind of trust is important, especially when the team might not understand how much this means to you and how much you have sacrificed to get to where you are.

Integrity is one of the most essential qualities a financial planning team must have when managing someone's life savings. You must find out if the advisory team you decide to work with has integrity. Ask the right questions, research the company, and search the team's personal social media pages (to see who they are when they're not in a suit and what they do when no one is watching). "How you do anything is how you do everything." This is your life savings, so who you trust to help you with it is a big decision.

Now, as promised, I will present my story about blueberries, which illustrates the Midwestern Millionaire's character traits very well.

Frozen Blueberries

I was at my parents' house one day and happened to open their deep freezer. After staring unbelievingly for half a minute, I realized the entire freezer chest was full of blueberries. The whole thing!

I asked my mother why she would do something like this, and she said: "Because they were on sale."

I definitely understand that "sale" concept. I'm the same way (family trait—the apple didn't fall far from the tree). I buy items on sale and save money when I can, because I work hard for my money, and I value it. I still had to challenge my mom, however, and press her for more information. She's in a great financial situation and wouldn't be set back by buying blueberries at full price (even in the quantity filling her freezer).

"It's the principle of the matter," she explained.

It's what she was taught throughout her years growing up. My mom came from a bigger family and was taught how to be frugal and to wisely preserve and conserve what she had. She has carried that mindset with her throughout her life. Just like almost every Midwestern Millionaire, she is naturally frugal.

What I have found after a lifetime of observing my mother's behaviors, traits, and values is that this type of money-saving purchase gives her joy. To save money on something she would have bought anyway delights her—like she's won. It is, in fact, the principle of the matter to her: Even though she can buy the blueberries at full price and not hurt financially because of it, she would rather save the money and consider it a win in her books for being frugal. I'm sure many of you reading this book share this trait.

This is the kind of Midwestern Millionaire care, attention, and diligence you want to deploy when it comes to managing and maximizing your life savings. It's the kind of attention and care we deploy for each client. That's why we work with those with Midwestern values, just like us.

Back to my mom for a moment. Sometimes I try not to encourage my mom about how well she's doing because she currently works with us at Peak Retirement Planning, Inc., as my executive assistant. It's a job she's good at and has experience with. She worked for the federal government in Columbus, Ohio for the top executives at the Defense Logistics Agency, which is a big deal. Here's the thing: I can't let her think she could retire, or I would lose a key employee. I'm joking, of course. I seriously love working with my mom. She quit her job to help me start this firm when I was twenty-five years old. That means the world to me.

People often ask what it's like working with my mom, and I tell them it's nothing new. She has been my assistant and been there for me all my life. Although she could retire, she enjoys the purpose of our mission that we have and is dedicated to serving others. Many Midwestern Millionaires also share that trait of wanting to have a purpose throughout all their years, including retirement.

Now, let's dive into the care, attention, and diligence that is needed and what Midwestern Millionaires must do now with their life savings to protect it.

—

PEAK RETIREMENT
• PLANNING, INC. •

READ

Read our Amazon bestselling books, "I Hate Taxes" and "Midwestern Millionaire".

Browse our articles that are featured in National Kiplinger publications for financial tips and more!

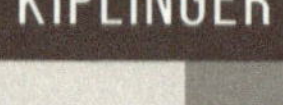

WATCH

Watch us weekly on the news where we discuss important retirement strategies.

Find us on YouTube, where we publish educational videos for those in or near retirement every week!

LISTEN

Listen online or on the radio to hear us discuss your top retirement concerns.

Tune in to our educational podcast "Joe Knows Retirement."

AUDIOBOOKS AVAILABLE

Narrated by Joe himself!

Scan the QR code to start listening!

About the Author

Joe F. Schmitz Jr., CFP®, ChFC®, CKA®, is the founder and CEO of Peak Retirement Planning, Inc., which was named the number one fastest growing private company in Columbus, Ohio, by Inc 5000 in 2025. Peak Retirement Planning, Inc. serves "Midwestern Millionaires" across the country with its popular 5 Pillar Approach to help clients grow and protect their wealth.

As a CERTIFIED FINANCIAL PLANNER™, Joe has passed a rigorous education program and certification exam to receive the CFP® designation. Joe has also received the Certified Kingdom Advisor (CKA®) designation, demonstrating that he has learned the finer points of retirement planning in accord with Christian principles. He has created a firm that helps his clients have a deep sense of purpose in how they steward their wealth. Joe got his start in the financial services industry in 2015. He graduated with a bachelor of science in finance and financial planning from Mount Vernon Nazarene University, where he also played basketball and ran track. Known as a thought leader in the industry, he is featured in Kiplinger twice a month and various TV news segments weekly. He is the author of the bestselling books *I Hate Taxes*, *Midwestern Millionaire*, and *The 2% Club*. You may have also seen Joe on YouTube, where he has one of the largest educational retirement planning channels for those in or near retirement.

SAVING FOR RETIREMENT IS LIKE CLIMBING A MOUNTAIN

It takes a long time and one wrong move can be disastrous. But building a nest egg and getting to the top of the mountain is only half the battle. The journey back down the mountain is even more dangerous—and it's where most losses occur.

In this book, Joe F. Schmitz Jr. shares a simple way to protect what you've worked so hard to create and to ensure your money makes it through the treacherous terrain called retirement. After reading this book, you'll appreciate and understand:

- How **Tax Planning** strategies can ensure you do not overpay in taxes

- Where **Investment Planning** can help you take less risk in retirement

- When **Income Planning** with a distribution plan can lead to success

- Why **Healthcare Planning** is nearly inevitable to plan for

- What **Estate Planning** documents and strategies must be in place

Saving for retirement is one thing. Enjoying retirement and making your money last is quite another. By following this proven process you'll be fully equipped to enjoy your trek down the mountain of retirement and will have taken every precaution to ensure a safe arrival.

You deserve to enjoy your retirement without worrying about risks, dangers, or loss. Read this book to learn how to protect your savings—and your family—using the 5 Pillars of a Peak Retirement plan.

Joe F. Schmitz Jr., CFP®, ChFC®, CKA®, is the founder and CEO of Peak Retirement Planning, Inc., which was named the number 1 fastest growing private company in Columbus, Ohio by Inc 5000 in 2025. Known as a thought leader in the industry, he is featured in Kiplinger twice a month and various TV news segments weekly. He is the author of the best-selling books *I Hate Taxes*, *Midwestern Millionaire*, and *The 2% Club*. You may have also seen Joe on YouTube, where he has one of the largest educational retirement planning channels for those in or near retirement.